Flinch of Song

Tupelo Press Annual First Book Award
now co-sponsored with the journal *Crazyhorse*

The Next Ancient World, Jennifer Michael Hecht
Selected by Janet Holmes

Miracle Fruit, Aimee Nezhukumatathil
Selected by Gregory Orr

Devoted Creatures, Bill Van Every
Selected by Thomas Lux

Everyone Coming Toward You, David Petruzelli
Selected by Campbell McGrath

Bellini in Istanbul. Lillias Bever
Selected by Michael Collier

Cloisters, Kristin Bock
Selected by David St. John

Flinch of Song, Jennifer Militello
Selected by Carol Ann Davis and Garrett Doherty,
co-editors of *Crazyhorse*

Published with the support of

COLLEGE *of*
CHARLESTON

home of the journal *Crazyhorse.*

Flinch
of
Song

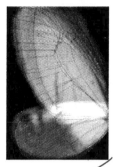

Jennifer
Militello

T|P

TUPELO PRESS
NORTH ADAMS, MASSACHUSETTS

Library of Congress Cataloging-in-Publication Data
Militello, Jennifer
Flinch of song : poems / Jennifer Militello. — 1st paperback ed.
p. cm. — (Tupelo Press First Book Award)
Summary:"Moving metaphorically from birth to death, including resignation and a
prayer for mercy, a poet grapples with human existence by conveying the smaller,
everyday tragedies of family and love" —Provided by publisher.
ISBN 978-1-932195-76-7 (pbk. : alk. paper)
I.Title.
PS3613.I53225F57 2009
811'.6—dc22

2009017237

Cover and text designed by William Kuch, WK Graphic Design.
Printed in the United States.
First paperback edition: October, 2009.

Tupelo Press
P.O. Box 1767, North Adams, Massachusetts 01247
Telephone: (413) 664–9611 / Fax: (413) 664–9711
editor@tupelopress.org / www.tupelopress.org
Telephone: (413) 664–9611 / Fax: (413) 664–9711
editor@tupelopress.org / www.tupelopress.org

Tupelo Press is an award-winning independent literary press that publishes fine
fiction, non-fiction, and poetry in books that are a joy to hold as well as read. Tupelo
Press is a registered 501(c)3 non-profit organization, and we rely on public support
to carry out our mission of publishing extraordinary work that may be outside the
realm of the large commercial publishers. Financial donations are welcome and are
tax deductible.

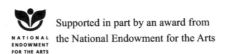

Supported in part by an award from
NATIONAL the National Endowment for the Arts
ENDOWMENT
FOR THE ARTS

For my mother and father

Contents

The genuine pain that keeps everything awake
is a tiny, infinite burn on the innocent eyes of other systems.
—Federico García Lorca

Manifestation /

So you have become several morning voices since
evening grew too deep to speak into. So you are
another, sheltering a little flask of sorrow, with
two eyes caged in wildness, lids too much like rainfall,

lashes a soprano's liquid pause. Since one must
worship the trees (their winter branches bones
in the fingers) and one must worship the earth
(astronomical as bodies mingled), I tell you to fall back

from the many windows beading a necklace
with their night. The world is always speaking hems
of dresses, evergreens, always speaking never.
The world is the jawbone of where we cannot go.

The snow has the embroider of calm dogs lying,
has you fallen long like rope among the flowers.
Its briar patch of handmade paper expresses
the blankness of thousands. Its fire, a hand

that hungers unlike anything, its bloodstream
spoken like a torture. You will understand flesh
better now, its fireflies deciphered, its clicking
rosary beads of wordless sound. When you open

your mouth, those few birds that fly out cast
a calcium of swans. They pass aquariums for fear
of watching at the window of another creature's life.
They change around your center like the rain.

The Museum of Being Born

The Museum of Being Born

I remember now. Something was chasing
blackbirds from my mouth. My hands
were willows or their speechless wives.

I remember morning like a feline thing
with a pelt gray-gloved as a mild girl's iris
or the sighing a highway does in its sleep.

Time grew bilingual. Roads so far along
the edge they were liquids still condensing.
The fog was graphite. The night B flat.

I had a complexion and her sonnets matured
to wax. I burned fertile with the thought
of death. I ate from a dish of camphor.

I woke to each streetlamp's liquor
at the bottom of the glass, the cold,
ornate lateness the neon diseases to light.

How small my gallop away from the dark,
how the seeds have the smallest fingers
I have ever felt in my eyes wanting

their way out. And off in the distance,
pain, an anvil for beating mere mongrels
into elegant beasts. Too late,

the soft unlathing, the not-yet grief
of loons. Love, the roost of writhing.
Futility, my little alone.

History of the Always Pain

When I was born, I woke in the bedrooms
of admirals. Now I want a sky so blue
it is arrows. I want to sleep under the jawline
of a town of balconies, to dream as

the desert in my elbow expands to my wrist,
until my arm is the only branch to grab
from the river to keep from drowning, my arm
already dead and dragging. Its weight

strains the metronome of my heart, and what is absent
makes the world what it is. Once,
I would ask you to enter churches, to dissolve
the wafer on the tongue, to light the short candles

so that they burned down quickly to the ash-like
sand. Now, the waterfall strikes with its tail
and drowns in its own finale. The impossible
never sleeps. Empty of pain, you place me

in the curled edge of the iris, partly
a hand held out, partly afraid, and let
my skin touch the dark star of the tarantula,
its notorious venom the next unruly source.

Passing for Red

It begins with the leftover drops on your dull shoes
vanishing the way you think each gesture might.

It begins with a shaker emptied of salt,
with the shabby remains of an ancient statue,

with a transparent dress of lisse. From there
it throws back severed starfish, shatters what's thick,

puts a crack in what's blind. If you swallow it
it will strike you, then crack each cooling mold.

If you inhale it, get down on your knees
and pray to the deity of compassion. She will

rescue you if there's a line of empty trashcans
in your yard, or gray paint flaking from your porch.

Unlike times of bankruptcy and war, there is less than nothing
to pose as advice. Keep as visible as a wristbone,

keep your organs in their dark chambers; if the air feels unclean
imagine your lungs. Direction is important to the sea,

gravity rules the moon, but there are no gods here.
Try passing for red, packing an unlit pipe for guidance,

leaving clear the failure to predict a world
in which each moment is a stoplight swinging in place.

The Objectless Place, an Ether Twist

The no one in my experience is the no one with a finger on the
trigger, with a hand on the gun, the nothing that has happened
since the cedar mill burned down and some places escaped
within its sootblack source. The lack of a village infects us. The
no one I envision could rip my heart out and does not suffer with
organs himself. The father I have never met but whose profile I
recognize when it comes together in the cellar of my eye from
the little pieces washed ashore of me bit by bit. His ache in the
algae, his mind the smashed syringe. The strength of his jaw in the
wash of sand. The closed pores of his daily lack of speech gleam
beautifully in any light. The other side of a bottomless, teething
lake is not impossible. The geese are not already extinct. It is not
the bare trees that make me wish for the many avenues of music,
but the knowing that they will grow leaves again until no longer
double-jointed, until all the choices are no longer frightening, until
they seem one green grasp when I imagine they exist.

History of Siblings

Once the home had been broken, we drank
from its stream which again went to shards
in our mouths. We set fire to its ashes

which reassembled into our bodies at once.
They became again the very erasure
in which the streets, the dipping of their

several necks, are clearly heard.
When we ran, we consumed the way back
to be sure we would never return. Lost in

the scatter, we hummed ourselves a song
once sung to us in a room the image
of porcelain. Those voices of secondhand smoke

dragged long in us. All the petals falling from
the same clear pause. And even if it seemed
a dream coming through, it became a reality

leaving. What kept us digging but
the brilliance tangling our woodgrained hair,
opening wind, its wide convertible.

Confusing Past with Passion

I swear it was summer: I was strung through
with light. Nothing offered shelter but the river
and a tremble of depth that kept us questioning.

And if our folds were full of wolves, you can imagine
the predators we feared. Sixteen swallows the same
as destination. An ordinary house on unordinary nights.

Now the river looks nothing like our skins. Its scales
mistaken for sunlight or blood, then becoming them.
Each gleams twice once left behind, its gold watch

hypnotic. New sadnesses ungather every time;
I've never known so many, such. Becoming boats
turned over, beached. Ribs bleached, blue once.

Sympathy/Wisdom

Someone let the dogs inside; I remember
they brought a brightness we recognized as blindness

and the slack chains twisted into augers' flights,
skinning the yard like the backbones of snakes.

A hand worked the softness until it softened.
What opened was broken, like voices

the color of a crow's eye blinking, the color
of a storm which has influenced the sea.

My grandmother took my hand beside
the shoreline's fuse a horse of flame burned

galloping down, the strength in her grip a darkening
which searched hungry and swallowed whole.

I felt her lengthened step extend past mine.
There was no stopping the world's leaving.

Allergic

My mother, sudden with bees. Skin swarming into
the one sad twine a road seems from this distance,
the fabric smokeless winter one can bend

to see the question break, the zero, the stalk
where it grows in the blood with the rhythm of lovers
who have nothing to lose, the cracked, inexpensive

wristwatch crystal of each wing working, a vast
collection of spectacles. She keeps still under
their dried groves, their redecorated, stemless lilies

and November's velvet cords. Her lips hisses,
a spill of starved machines, her adrenaline lips,
her barbed wire lips, in her one eye gravel

willowing, fracture, fronds of singe. The hours
like twelve tarnished, interior birds. Countless
spores. Intravenous. My mother is sudden with bees.

I Have Never Stood Outside a House Burned Down

The light is a lengthy rope uncoiling. It is only
a thin arm holding autumn back. It is my ability
to remember the footsteps going, and to let

the sadness net all else. The incoming light is just
some skin dreaming, or seahorses delicate like they
shouldn't live. Its architecture is broken by the slant

of my hip or the way the sun won't fall as the clouds
roll in. Broken by a body, my voice on the blackness,
bareback. My voice the ragged wings of autumn's way

of dragging branches across the room. One could almost
crush in the lack of sky. One could almost hold
a hawk that keeps landing on the ungloved hand.

How the seahorses bend their heads and become
delicate. How the seahorses are the standing
some way off we do to twine the wind around

what we have and call it substance, though
we know it is wind. Saying, hear what
the walls hear: a voice thrown, a child

singing to herself while her father sleeps
nearby. Place the half that has not been broken
against the half that has.

Game with Hours Galloping, a Garland

The children set out. They watch the chamomile
grow up between their fingers and dream that
they are born of wood. Tentless, their slight bodies

dry like lavender. What irises and songs
in the wasp's spun nest, in the lids of stars
and grains of wheat, in the sand's pronouncements

through each child's hands. The tentacles of breath
in their tethered horses frost the dwindled fires.
The children set out, lamenting as limbs lament,

swimming as schools do, their quivers dyed with
the ochers of the sea and filled with undersides of thorns.
Insect wings ask questions in the underbrush

and the children answer with the snowdrifts they
imagine, with a kind of white, with tiny wrists and
tiny voices, with the lambs of their long long joy.

Manifestation

Where you survive is an early indication of how
you will break: with autumn scathing: like the hem
of a skirt brushing back wildflowers from the skin.

Even while evening sends messages through the birds
unknotting their way through a sky of rivers
toward a sky colored over with paper and twine.

This is the twin fish of the self speaking,
never knowing it was growing emptier
with the trying, never knowing it was turning

in the saddle to look back over the dunes
at the hoof prints' small torches burning in sand,
to cut out of you a tender margin

around which to repair anguish: you are
not too young to remember the days
when half the challenge was to remain.

Dark, Godless Reactions

After Days Not Found

If we aren't yet starving, we will be soon.
You go on and on to find entire leaves.
How many chimes come forward from

the pearl-spined gardens. More than can be counted,
enough to send hours I have not yet learned
to pronounce far off, into a corner plot of land.

The constellation of our prints won't show
the way out. The collapse of them entrances us,
until we become distracted by where they lead.

So crumbled are the evenings that even sleep is ruin.
The shadow of the mountain makes the mountain
small. Stories change with the traveling.

Last night I wore a shift of stars, buttoned
at the sleeve. I was following you, then
you were following me. There were a number

of appropriate responses, and I couldn't
stop having them. The stars wheeled in me,
merging where the just-dusk grew botanical.

Now your called voice returns to take us by the throat.
You cross the broken river with the crush
of your boot and rarely turn back to me.

I am just over your shoulder, or still at your side.
Flowers are straw; you are fragile or fierce.
There is no prayer I know the whole of.

The Zero to Breaking

It was the contagion that woke me
while I was feigning sleep. The cold
of what we held close was there in the room,

a waterlight bicycle with a fender chrome
and rivergreen. And you were the pilot
of this bone hawk, uncatchable brightness,

this distance, not speed. I kept breaking.
I kept remembering when there wasn't a day
to light darkness by. I kept knowing.

Even now, the fragile moments continue weaving
their wicker chairs. They must know the places
they fill in me. Each small sound must carry

small, like an injured bird in the hand.
It wants a hinge. It burns like heaven.
It won't be seen as an unloved thing.

An undiscovered attic lays like a tool
of clay and night behind your stranger's
face. Admitting it is a little stitch

undone no matter how I mend it. Instead,
I scatter milkweed. I wake while dreaming.
I set the stolen horses free.

The Window Painted Shut

I remember the seagulls were brides.
If only I could so perfectly remember the time

kept by your eyes, such bright hours each,
such animals when left to themselves.

There were our only bones laced into other selves,
but there were also soft men working in secret.

When you touched me I thought I heard
the wild crane of the rest of my life

shooting its loom, its labor, bitter but good.
I didn't know the white light was my white thigh

reflecting a sharpness of spurs. I didn't know
you lived by the wishes of your hands.

When you touch me I become a child I see
hiding, a smallish wind, a stifled cry.

From Panama, From Ashes

You spent three days dug into your self-dug grave,
listening for the gears that pull the doors
shut, listening from your tender cell,
every hour growing false, lying to you

in the thunder voice only an ear pressed
to its final ground can discern. Night and day
were two sides of the enemy's face, bringing you
into the undergrowth of patience, the patience

of a heart stopped by the amber glass
of an orange sky. Your heart's fire
grew a sky of thorns, the branches of fallen trees,
a hearth made whole with broken bits of other stone.

There was no signal when you returned, no volley
of gunfire, no unbraiding smoke; only the quiet
former light leaking out to the hospital's whiteness,
a basin of light you discovered all day as it fell.

Something about your blood draining the soil dry
rooted you to something other than the fading
that made death. It's what stayed with you
when the helicopter chopped through to a future,

what kept blackness fasting like an unfortunate town;
it's the silo that brought you back. Some jungle
ate out what was the whole of you with a hunger
that let pain equal one million ants attacking

and the absence of flesh. That lack
threatens me when we embrace. I feel
the cold boil of castanets, the kisses of rattlesnakes,
an emptying of teeth from my bronze shield of calm.

Infliction

You are the fields I make which spill a little
into my hands, then spill a little out of them.

I am the echoes you hear which number
like my hair and move similarly, with some freedom,

with some restraint, the wide illumination within
a river's text. There was another time like this,

and yet nothing resembles this, ever.
We sit at the table of long nights to feast.

It is morning before your eyes open, spending
their blue on the room. They have a color the reach

of the sigh of a train. They make corridors
I hide into: harp in the wind's voice, drum

in my throat. They make a solitude sharpened
toward the purr of some falling, not snow,

but enough to cover this gape in the land.
A thin film on still waters. Miracle. Trick.

Recipe for the Motorcyclist's Leather Gloves

Prepare threads of oxblood, vanishingly rare.
Remember a gray room going more gray

as if the color of his irises were fading, his single eye
diminishing toward a distant flock of birds,

the sky scraping its radioactivity
at his hydraulic bones. Use three strands

of his windblown hair from which yesterday's nests
are weaving. As it is, he stands with the neck

of a smashed bottle in his fist to counter
the transition from the road. Seconds pirouette.

No flat sand can match his alchemy.
Cut from a choir of kerosene glances

a root-colored interruption in the world's
explosive blooms. Walk, a pauper, among molecules,

along the coast of your caught self
opening close to the scales of a milk snake,

its coiling and tropical skin. The city has never
seemed so papal with its occasional white dove;

its landscape particularly says the emergency
of things. Rats abandon ships. The past thins

to ash on the hands. Dream its circadian rhythm,
some slither slipping down the thin winghusks

of hours as if this life were sudden rhinestones
discovered only as one comes apart.

Aprilia

Lately, the light dies of grief. Even leaves seem
starlings. We keep chasing through statues, through skin,

through the brutal in your forearms, your hair black
as birds. We follow the path worn in grass by some

captive animal, until clouds gain distance's same red edge.
Your shoulders husk mouths out of which languages

tangle and fail, and crying is not enough sleep.
And night is a wire. And earth is a sign.

I begin to let the scent of forsythia get to me.
I let you put the door in only, the passing in speed,

the start to dark godless reactions. What once dozed
in the cold stalls of an open barn, breathing a cotton

clean as milk, now chooses avenues more dried petals
than black flies. Now an early child practices late magic;

you flush an accident of birds into several curtains
parting, to let morning through, to complicate the trees.

Reunion

The woman, meanwhile, is a sea-wind rising; the man
is only a tattered coat. Bright things are clipped
from themselves sharply, paltry cities, burned out light.

This, the third draft of loving you. This, a healed leg
twisted in place. In descending we are lessening: in surrender
we are small. Can't you see we are torn with the one tusk

left to winter. Can't you understand enough to want
untroubled sleep. A crumb of nothing comes between;
you look back from the surface of what is submerged.

The woman, meanwhile, is a call for the roses; the man
is a call for the reeds. From here they can't define
what might conquer the midnight pull and papered ache.

Among the dangers of hungers of others, we are much
too thin. Among geese flying low in late November,
the ragged air breathing, an applause swept of wings.

Taking Care

Since the trick is separateness, I withdraw.
I dig a well, I work bellows, I weld.
I break wild mares for the bridle and bit.

I take lovers who are strangers and like experiments
failed we create wrong-colored flame and taint
those elements least stable. I remember well

the shore of forest. I say, how beautiful
the ruined barn, the late blade of candidness.
I mistake the cathedral for a sodium light

sifting down from how it lingers, everywhere
and sometimes always, a mist of linen,
a hay-sweet sight. I notice dandelions

become exact around us. I dream myself
a guest of the world, its crouched cities,
its African plains. I dream dolphins

to confuse with water while swimming.
I extricate the trellis from the blackberry bramble.
I dream two trees so close they complain.

The Conductor's Last Call Before Leaving

Somewhere, sailboats smear the sea behind them.
Somewhere, it rains. There is a somewhere
you enter into calmly, without looking back.

This loss is as librarian as the yards
of junked cars, upholstery gutted and windows
rough with forgetting. It's been an hourly collection

of years, and this cracked announcement
is the day ripping into a net of language that so often
tangles in itself. It's been days, and still

the sun drags its bad leg. Its spreading bruise
purples two entire rooms and whatever
they contain. When will I stop filling

my ear's pitcher with the words inside
the words? You have left me with a cathedral
of trees and no church to speak of.

The unpinning braids of factory smoke,
the moth that keeps landing inside me.
When I listen, every cricket's leg is partnered,

making me a shadow touching no other shadow,
near to two cooled tracks that never meet for miles,
one my very single spoke, my very spine.

North, with the Ingredients for Rain

Now the harness won't hold. Now an edgewater,
half lilac, half lupine, takes the place of an afterlife.

Once, you were Spanish rain that dangerously fell.
Other times need other thunder. With the plow's

low motion in the throat, it is the murmur that wounds
as its strangle persists. This moving chooses

when it chooses death: a sudden illness, a slight limp.
Meanwhile, I dream a silt that kills me, sunless as water

but built by your hands. The deer are the aching
that comes out to feed, its different kinds of lying still.

A Thorn in the Softest Part of the Hand

What you call history is my whisper
against what could come. Things have
become night-terrible, things we might not notice

are multiplying among their cinders.
There is no station for stopping, no sun
so overripe. There are feathers without any birds.

And while a tambourine keeps loosening joy
somewhere in your foreground, already the drum's skin
we thrum inside is an empty trough. Every step

feels its missing sister. What can be done
with such willful light? Already blackberries
bead a knotted necklace of my blood,

weave of me a blanket smelling strongly of smoke,
a warning as velvet as the nostrils of horses,
while a parrot's black tongue is lifting.

What We No Longer Know

Whether the severe theater of your shadow
breaks into ravens or is broken into crows.

Whether morning makes a list of last night's weapons,
or if warmth is any kind of reminder.

Whether the night is a wide car worth driving.
Whether angry water makes martyrs of the stones.

When exactly fear, crushed by your feet
as you entered the room, gave off its slight odor.

When exactly you opened your mouth
and I saw the teeth of a laid trap.

If pieces of ourselves are darker when apart.
How my skin healed if it was never cut.

Whether open doors everywhere ever open further.
When two voices at once become the same voice twice.

(start)

I had the clock in my hands + I went through the door + the day
was lightning + the door was a clock.

time held you like water time did not hold me + the clock was a
door I went through + without you time was water +

you + a paper where some complacence was torn

where our hearts met and our rib cages met and our eyelids felt
like water + I was where the door ended a stairwell.

was like light + I felt you go long before I held the clock + hands
until they were still I held + your hands under water.

you + the computer hum of your nights alone + a black place
waiting to be spread more thin.

I walked out + there was little else to go + there was lightning
like a water + time + electricity filled our hearts their beating +

was so loud we walked in time apart + the footsteps so broad
the water was where + we could not go a clock =

one hand faster than the other around. one hand like lightning.
the other, alone.

Manifestation

Take your ceramic waist, your waist
the taste of porcelain, and nudge back
into my nights. There is a quiet I excavate

in waiting for you. Drink from my softness,
its anemic wound. Drink from the cup
of my hand and I will show you

a broader eye than this. For once
I drank from the ribs of weeping,
from a ship designed for speed at sea.

Once I sipped and the salt of my lips
mixed with the violence I shed. There
in the cup bloomed a drop of blood,

blossoming, a single drop, a parachute
for men. Your memories are worse injuries
than this. Hear the stems of me broken off

by the footsteps at night, see the bleed of me
lighten like a late horizon and return only
by covering the world. From the flounders

swimming, windmill patterns. Their lanterns
draw a chariot we might ride beyond, to blend
together in a hand of black, in a bird painted

of water. At the bottom of the water
only a silt made of crossing it, only
a courtyard stirred by the animals that drink.

Identity Narrative

Identity Narrative

Do not eat from October's black hand, O my situation.

Are you still. Listen. Innocence: a seam to be stitched or split with
a throw of omens. I lay me down, my soul to keep. I have sown my
amen in the earth.

Sometimes, I live in the open. My heartbeat a lamb, my heartbeat I am
bleeding from the mouth a heartbroken rain. The thin inches time
will give me winter as I stand and watch. The small in me has anthems
made of time's mouth made of thousands of beads.

I will read my more childish self to sleep. She will use locusts only
for as long as they robe the fields with the feeding they were meant
for. She will nest where bats nest, set curtains to burning, place a
marker beside my name so that I might return.

Her heart, made of shale, lies in the mouth of a pious man. Its verses
are stalls that keep the wind ceaseless. Its lamps cry light in the shape
of young lovers as they two-step through the four rooms of God.

Living Where the Halyards Can Be Heard

The only identity I know is alone in the sigh's
bright wilderness, with workings one can take apart
and still not understand. What the veins say

is a whole species of distress. One can hear the cold
in the mind's eaves and cloaks. I used to think
significance; now I feel it in the temperature-sensitive

nerves of my teeth, fascinated by sadness or
fascinated by the sad woman and her glass shadow
breaking to travel as the satellite I would have been

had I wasted away or played dead and woken
in the road. I wouldn't say a downpour just
to hear it rain. To burn and say, You made me

burn. To lack and have at once. We are laymen
at the oars. At the bottoms of the harbor
where we beg, star-like, half-hearted, half

heaven, half hail, with our green eyes made
slightly of depth, coils and coils of rope.
The only identity I know is what bitter hemispheres

I am made from. A life, its far amnesia, its archipelagos
perishing. The rest is a gauze re-creation:
morning like a bride left at the altar,

the single lost earring in a lover's matched pair.
The seagull's cry like the year none of the dogs
came back. We knew we would find their bones.

A Thunderstorm Reminds Me of My Convictions

Its blue cathedral is trembling into the marrow
of my mouth. Its sharp houses split open

every string, then still into the trotting
of rain. I live with unburied bones

that brown instead of bleaching. Somehow
I am separate from this. I will die

and then grow old. The wheat and I will bend
to different rivers. The wind will also

brush my hair. The trees have already untethered
their Appaloosas of shadow and shine.

If I bear a daughter she will not find me
among low ceilings and half-black veils.

Each of my heartbeats unlocks an asylum.
There is good hunting. There is terrible joy.

Self-Portrait as Someone Else

She is the parlor that collects smoke's lacing,
its breakfront filled with the cut-glass sound

of a key turning. She has the impatient strength
of fishermen, with things kept out

and other things kept in. She is allergic
to natural light. She keeps her choir disguised

as a set of criminals; she gathers angry bouquets
to bring when she calls. She carries sections

of smoldering rope for the African herdsmen
of her intimate dreams. She collects viceroy

when she should imagine rain. Her name is the train
that leaves tonight for an imagined destination.

Instructions to a Portraitist

Add to me a mechanical voice, the smell
of the heavens because they smell of the earth,
and what would hydrogen-react with past forms of us

falling. Add to me the removal: let the blood
that follows bead. Look half at me, half at
the long grass color the sky is beginning to have,

beauty's poisonous reptile sleeping in your hand.
If I wear a gemstone, make its thousands laugh.
Don't think. You must reshape me as the fabrics

grow weak. Otherwise, I come out colorless
and afraid. Add to me a long stretch of wetlands
and the dying off of birds. Invent me teeth to

bite with, scars to leave, the places you would maim
already in my eyes as atmospheres the edges
whisper, profiles I have let swan, all the children

you will later be made to believe in,
their lineless fists and brows of silver lakeness.
The gunshot, the cricket song, irises of steam.

One Side of the Story

Fearless of grief, I go white and rather.
I cube as my patient sings precisely.
I spend her sickness like the torn dollar lost.

When I see my bent outline resembles
her shadow, I go folded in critical freedom,
gold of an iceberg. The menu says,

eat crying and nothing that's hot. Sandwich
the gap. Don't let yourself be narrowed
by a dark impossible wing. I am asking

questions in my sleep while a noiseless room
can't answer. Solitary? I wonder. Ornamented?
Once the windows open, the cure will whistle in.

This Is Elementary

I burnt my skin. I burnt its jar of flax.
I burnt the vast remains nostalgia had.
I burnt the fix. I burnt the drug.
I burnt in fits. I burnt in starts.
I burnt the burned up hearts of knowing.
I burnt the long gone hearts of lost.
I burnt the cost. I burnt the impostor
I thought was first. The only hunger
I thought was thirst. The silo-
white leviathans of voice.

I masked the past with images of health.
I masked the statues at my heart.
I: amputated inkwell bone, tired
of a thing, my soil a natural
pierce of shadows and shattered bottles
and uncut girls. Intricates of Satan.
Meanwhile, a world. I: a razor blade
of rooftops at dusk. The body
of lovers in my mouth. I have burned up
well, a wasp-husk close to winter.

True or false: it is ever enough.

Flinch

Murder is what we seem, deep in such black feathers.
Night, a revolver emptying rounds, sends us so far

we are gone for good, suffocating with the strings
on the sack pulled taut, seized like an oilless engine.

Because I burn in symptoms though the illness
has been cured, I hear hooves which, galloping,

drag a wing and crave a length, drop open
paper fans of air like the storm still gathering

a long way off. Because I fill with injury,
I strike the child, I grip the blind man's cane.

Ask me to promise, I will promise you this:
not looking, we can see for miles. Not sleeping,

we can sleep. The moth at the screen will beat
its wings, twin throats of torture in a flinch of song.

There's No Such Thing as a Typical Day

Once my waters remember other days,
I am out in the field, accompanying

a chronic shift in shadow and shine. I try
to measure the effect of light on the armor of a figure

when there is armor, a figure, light. I keep
hearing my neighbor cough from her wall,

from her lung full of dark. The first bars of laughter come;
I will never recover. An ingress is sweetened

by bouvardia or larkspur. Without mystery,
a ballet dancer can barely lift, a man

can barely stand idle in the window
of a bathtub showroom, haloed by the tiled light.

Suddenly, hunger seems better than being full.
The sheriffs depend on their tempered tin stars.

Strange how the story empties like a coat sleeve.
Strange not to hear some insect's wing.

Waking is when you realize some man is dying
or about to be hung. His moments become lakes

of constellation, more darkness between
than stars I see from the back of my underfed horse.

Slow the Bleeding

Emptiness never was my mother. I only called it home
with wishing, when long ago the bread
ran out, and my animals could no longer share

their house with childhood. Now, from far inside
lightning, I finally see. There's nothing to be made
of this place. Darkness is determined to stay

familiar, and if I do the little singing, I will
not need light. My doves flee evening by filling
the thick branches where it first gathers.

I come ashore at forgetfulness. I go into
the sea when the sun is just right: into
my hand goes gleaming until all my thousand

mouths are opened, though I don't know what
they want. Emptiness was a world followed
closely by the locusts, though it already had

their hunger. Now, when there are animals here,
I imagine them, though they are hiding. I drink
at the exhaustion this neighborhood makes.

My animals recognize light yellower than an eye,
streets dead leaves are sweeping, houses
spilling blackbirds as if they were seeds.

Please understand how painful this is, when
the vultures can't stand the waiting, when
the wolves can come because there is no world.

Manifestation

Now, without the never gardens, release
my sparks for the moments they exist. Extend
your hand, extend the songs of my beneath.

Flush me from underbrush, drag me through
the quarries—I don't know what this feeling is.
I run there and opening up in me is dark.

I press my palm to the window in the hope
it will read my Braille. A silkworm spinning
in a small glass jar, I build my small way out:

the wind. The city lights are smearing lives
around you as if you were the still thing.
Then somehow the body is ours, the center

causing only ripples, a meniscus over the way
you venture from the woods with the cancellation
of your eyes consuming everything. The way

you turn them to the world's other side
and it is night. The weep of rust among
your veins, the mouth spilled like emerging.

Impossibly, the parks rise up in us.
I keep hearing from the woods a belief
in wind as if there must be a belief in something.

The Last Burning Room

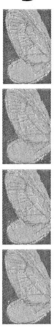

A Summary of Roots

I am done being sturdy, of bones.
I braid the small billow I am.

I assume nothing. Not the whole day
idle as wine in the glass. Not the heart,

a flounce of took roses. Not even
elegy, a metaphor for what.

Once the world was a womb
where I broke my throat with

trying to say. My mother's blood
was my blood running beads all through

the garden, while the body took on
a crossroads' weight. I opened my palm

for the first time: sight. Polluted
with the stigmata of briefly alone,

pressed like lilac in an unthick book,
an aspirin in the mouth of pain.

Answering Fear As If It Were a Question

In a unit of time, in a violence of sleep,
I first saw all the tiny murders in rain,
all the wartime verses: rain leading children

into the classroom of looking, into
the being afraid. Rain chipping its way
into the apple trees, into the mouths of rivers.

Stop, says the hypnosis. I cannot stop.
I've been thinking slivers of loneliness into
a handsewn shroud, thinking my toy heart

to ticking. Lying in bed at night, rain's
lonely sopranos opened in the palm like swimmers,
a mere lisp of dried flowers in the wind.

All the verbs are ceaseless dioramas
of its wounds. Last night, the raindrops
opened where I felt my mouth, into

flesh-electric briars that said, breathe in.
This dark bulb being born is your sight.
Let it trample you beyond all recognition.

Last night, I dreamed for the first time since.
I dreamed in concrete. I dreamed in wool.
I must have slept for years.

Questions of Perception

Must the years like lilies own us with their air
and with their molting fountains.

Must there be birds singing and birds evading song
while the wheat keeps asking its answerless mane.

The marching of wagons of petals is a sign
that the mills of our eyes will continue to churn,

to cross the earth, to brick among its cinders.
Must we understand the equivalent,

what blue looks like as we speak about black,
as ghosts lie alone with the traffic of ghosts.

Must these fields fill with the pulse of us,
with children who risk braiding bitter with sweet.

Roam Season

September arrives in a dark-windowed car,
its drones purring a lurch of wingless light,
candled, jawless, clean. Our limbs seem

the origin of apathy; nearby, winter armies
sleep. These are the long nocturnal hours
when relatives stand watch, when the parlors

are upholstered. All light is a trick
of drapery. On the hull of Eden, we have been
overturned. What we recall is the dark

and dried: sterling women, unsalvaged cars,
a parakeet grave covered with crabapples.
Gatherers once, we marked the perfumed smoke

between seasons, the rough sensations, ice
incomplete and floating. Now, bent bodies damage
the way we'd expect, heed what our slow breath

says: discard the small paper cups of childhood,
the cold, the notion you must take to have.
Go down to the river with your whole life.

Until We Have No Children

And the loveliness goes hand in hand with the graveyard,
if only at this time of year. No airplane or insects
or afterthought. No place for happening things.

Out of all the pigeons that rise up at once,
the one becomes a lantern. The only lanterns
are made of late cocoons, and of the roaming,

and of the eye. Even the sky must remember itself
as it comes through the leaves, crimson
with its own incredible hold. Even the fearful

must learn to fear; there must be light by which
to darken rooms, with shoulders unlike shoulders,
hands unlike hands. There must be jars

fired to be broken, napkins folded, checks
canceled, children crying in the street. There
must be motels to make one think of loneliness.

But, no. It's autumn. Time to hear the clear bell,
heavy bell, above the bent oxen. Nothing
resembles the lovers like their dove-like necks.

Resignation

How nudity looks on the laundry line and
on the body. How there is dust, though not the kind

the wind kicks up. Once, the stars would eat
holes through our hunger; we were lilies then,

with both the stringbean root and each serene lake.
We could cross our arms over the sarcophagi

of our bodies. We could prepare for faithlessness.
Now, every white shirt is a surrender; the ash

of last daylight leaves artifacts forgotten.
Often, there is no warning. There are only

winter boats to groan and twist rope
against clocks that grind and do not tick.

The Museum of Being, Ended

Bury me fiction, bury me wings,
bury me a stain won't fade, bury me
a sun torn of all its petals,
the mortally tuned, the never tangled.
Bury me a necessary blood.

Bury me beetle. Bury me fate.
Bury me as you slept, your hands,
as sudden as crazy as weak.

Bury me not enough handfuls of wheat,
bird-eaten seeds, with all the mouthfuls
of bitter liquid I could not swallow again.

Bury me a rainy afternoon.

Bury me on the threshold of all things,
waning. A glance, a hand, feel me
slowly like a wind, now in the trees,
now in your hair, now a word
too small for all this *here;*
bury me a blurring of skins.

Bury the moon, its mottle in me,
bury me the body were a fog of crickets
singing, the song of grasping tendons,
were made of fine incisions.

Bury me elegiac and the seep.
An architecture that waits to strike me down,
has order on its side, and the hounds of nowhere.

Bury me shallow, bury me shriek, bury me
speaking low sounds into unfamiliar rooms.

With a left foot dragging slightly.
With boil. With stormlight.
With a closing of lips.

Azrael Speaks

Nothing is made of wind, but the wind is made
of wasps caught between the window and the screen.

Welcome their weave of brightness as sleeping:
not revealing or perfect, alchemical or whole.

The twenty-second pane shows someone dreaming.
Without me, your arms will bruise. Row them

toward the murmur behind my original words.
This will hinge open like a shell if you let it.

How late it is: the floorboards are the color
of sunset, the lullaby you recognize twists in

among our roots. How intricate the wind.
How everything comes, and wearing white.

Miserere

Raw materials, have mercy on us.

Life is a ladder at the last burning room.
The burning is burning no matter how sweet.

Day keeps circling like a dog to sleep.
Dandelions hanging with their parasols of dust.

May we despair by their dim cloth.

May our hands grow into ghosts of the open, the whole,
birds which land separately but fly up all at once.

May treetops weave a crown of thorns.

Grief unbuttoning its high-collared dress.
Change as a heron that strikes at the lake.
Death at the heels, herding.

Wind as a skin in that it passes.

May it rain.

May we rest between failures.

Acknowledgments

Grateful acknowledgment is made to the editors of the following journals, in which these poems first appeared:

AGNI Online: "A Summary of Roots"
The Bellingham Review: "History of Siblings"
Black Warrior Review: "Roam Season"
Crazyhorse: "There's No Such Thing as a Typical Day," "A Thorn in the Softest Part of the Hand"
Denver Quarterly: "The Objectless Place, an Ether Twist"
Green Mountains Review: "Manifestation" ("Now, without the never gardens…")
The Greensboro Review: "Instructions to a Portraitist"
Gulf Coast: "Infliction," "The Museum of Being Born"
Hotel Amerika: "Aprilia," "(start)"
Icarus: "From Panama, From Ashes"
Indiana Review: "Resignation"
The Journal: "Flinch," "One Side of the Story," "Passing for Red," "The Window Painted Shut"
The Laurel Review: "Answering Fear As If It Were a Question," "Game with Hours Galloping, a Garland"
Mid-American Review: "After Days Not Found," "I Have Never Stood Outside a House Burned Down"
New Orleans Review: "Identity Narrative," "Miserere"
The New Republic: "Manifestation" ("So you have become…")
The Paris Review: "A Thunderstorm Reminds Me of My Convictions," "History of the Always Pain"
Prairie Schooner: "Allergic," "Reunion"
Quarterly West: "Sympathy/Wisdom," "The Zero to Breaking," "Taking Care"
Salt Hill: "The Conductor's Last Call Before Leaving"
Verse: "Confusing Past with Passion," "North, with the Ingredients for Rain"
The Virginia Quarterly Review: "Slow the Bleeding," "Until We Have No Children," "What We No Longer Know"

"Manifestation" ("So you have become . . .") appeared in the 2004 exhibition *Artists in the Studio: 30 Years at The Millay Colony for the Arts* at the Albany International Airport in Albany, New York, juried by John Ashbery.

"Answering Fear As If It Were a Question" and "The Museum of Being Born" were also featured on the *Verse Daily* website.

Thank you to the Millay Colony for the Arts and the Hambidge Center for the Creative Arts and Sciences for the gifts of time and place, and to Writers at Work for the fellowship that helped make this work possible. Thank you also to my teachers: Lucie Brock-Broido, Fred Chappell, Stuart Dischell,

Mekeel McBride, Alan Shapiro, and Charles Simic, and to the readers and supporters of this manuscript in its various forms: Heidi Czerwiec, John Gallaher, Matthew Guenette, Dionisio Martinez, Elizabeth Powell, Jim Schley, and Christina Veladota. And special gratitude to Jeffrey Levine, Carol Ann Davis, and Garrett Doherty for selecting the book for the Tupelo Press/*Crazyhorse* First Book Award.

Other Books from Tupelo Press

This Nest, Swift Passerine, Dan Beachy-Quick
Cloisters, Kristin Bock
Modern History, Christopher Buckley
Psalm, Carol Ann Davis
Orpheus on the Red Line, Theodore Deppe
Spill, Michael Chitwood
Then, Something, Patricia Fargnoli
Calendars, Annie Finch
Do the Math: Forms, Emily Galvin
Other Fugitives & Other Strangers, Rigoberto González
Keep This Forever, Mark Halliday
Inflorescence, Sarah Hannah
The Us, Joan Houlihan
Red Summer, Amaud Jamaul Johnson
Dancing in Odessa, Ilya Kaminsky
Ardor, Karen An-hwei Lee
Dismal Rock, Davis McCombs
Biogeography, Sandra Meek
At the Drive-In Volcano, Aimee Nezhukumatathil
The Beginning of the Fields, Angela Shaw
Selected Poems, 1970–2005, Floyd Skloot
Nude in Winter, Francine Sterle
Embryos & Idiots, Larissa Szporluk
Archicembalo, G.C. Waldrep
The Book of Whispering in the Projection Booth,
                              Joshua Marie Wilkinson
Narcissus, Cecilia Woloch
American Linden, Matthew Zapruder

See our complete backlist at www.tupelopress.org